How Many Spots Have I Got?

Lauren A. McCabe

illustrated by
Nancy Pelham Foulke

Text copyright © 2006 by Lauren A. McCabe
Illustrations copyright © 2006 by Nancy Pelham Foulke
All rights reserved. No part of this book may be used or reproduced in any manner or form whatsoever, electrical, mechanical, including photocopying, recording, or by an information storage and retrieval system without written permission, except in the case of brief quotations embodied in critical articles and reviews. For information please address the publisher:

Our Child Press
P.O. Box 4379
Philadelphia PA 19118-8379
email: ourchildpress@aol.com
http://www.ourchildpress.com

Library of Congress Cataloging-in-Publication Data
McCabe, Lauren A.
    How many spots have I got? / by Lauren A. McCabe ; illustrated by Nancy Pelham Foulke. p. cm.
    Summary: Chester Bartholomew Spot, a young ladybug, asks the other animals how many spots he has.
  ISBN 1-893516-02-4 (hardcover)
    [1. Ladybugs - Fiction. 2. Animals - Fiction. 3. Individuality - Fiction. 4. Stories in rhyme] I. Foulke, Nancy Pelham, ill. II. Title.

PZ8.3.M47833725How 2005
[E]–dc22
                                                              2005047776

Printed in Hong Kong

To Bob
   for believing in me
      • Lauren •

To Hugh
   who understands
      about spots
         • Nancy •

In a field by a farm on a bright sunny day,
A ladybug was born in the ladybug way.
His mom named him Chester Bartholomew Spot.
She brought him up well, and she loved him a lot!
He had all kinds of questions about all kinds of things,
Including how many spots he had on his wings.

He asked his dear mom to lend him a hand.
You see, there are no mirrors in Ladybug Land.
"I just have to know is it a little or a lot?
Please won't you tell me how many spots have I got?"

His mom thought for a moment, not quite sure what to say,
"Son, that is something you must learn for yourself someday."
Well, someday is too long for a young ladybug's mind,
So he set out on his own to see what he could find.

He came upon an old frog in great distress,
His tongue stuck in a can – what a terrible mess!

"Mr. Frog," said Chester, "I will help set you free,
If you promise not to make your next meal out of me."

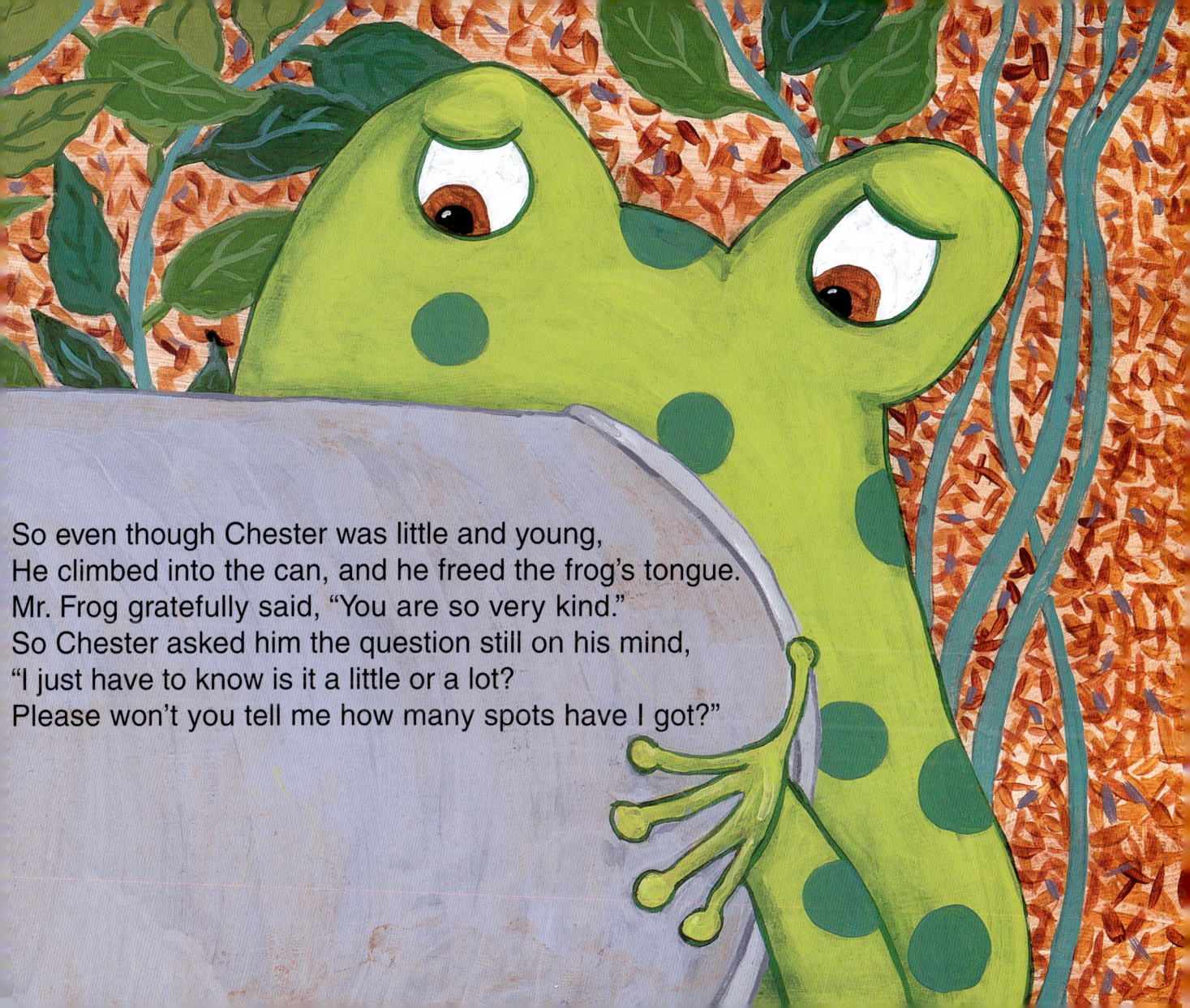

So even though Chester was little and young,
He climbed into the can, and he freed the frog's tongue.
Mr. Frog gratefully said, "You are so very kind."
So Chester asked him the question still on his mind,
"I just have to know is it a little or a lot?
Please won't you tell me how many spots have I got?"

The frog answered Chester, "Oh, you have a whole bunch!
But you'd better move on, it's almost time for my lunch."
Now, Chester was quite wise, though still in his youth.
He suspected the frog wasn't telling the truth.
So he set out once more on his spot finding quest.
Until he found the answer, he would simply not rest.

He saw Mama Rabbit with all of her brood,
And said, "Pardon me, I hate to be rude.
I just have to know is it a little or a lot?
Please won't you tell me how many spots have I got?"

Mama Rabbit was scolding her bunnies and shouting their names, "Son, can't you see, I'm much too busy for games?"

Chester counted the bunnies, but the number was high.
He finally gave up and then said with a sigh,
"Mama Rabbit, you must be incredibly smart,
For how else could you be able to tell them apart?"

Mama Rabbit let out a joyful sound.
She laughed so hard she fell to the ground.
"You've made me laugh. You've given me a lift.
Some days for mommies, that's a wonderful gift."

She gave him a hug and a kiss on the cheek,
"Now go off and find all the answers you seek."
Chester had to find out, he just didn't know how.
When he saw up ahead – a big spotted cow.

The cow was a rich creamy white with big black dots.
At last, thought Chester, someone who can appreciate spots!
"I just have to know is it a little or a lot?
Please won't you tell me how many spots have I got?"

The cow answered Chester with an annoyed little pout,
"Spots, what are they? I don't know what you are talking about."
Oh no, thought Chester, this simply can't be.
"By the way, Mrs. Cow – you have three."

Frustrated and ready to throw in the towel,
Chester remembered, Aha! The Wise Old Owl.
He found the old owl perched high in a tree,
And said, "Please kind sir, won't you help me?
I just have to know is it a little or a lot?
Please won't you tell me how many spots have I got?"

The owl looked down; then he thought for a while.
He looked Chester in the eye and said with a smile,
"Dear son, you are so young and so small,
But the truth is that you have no spots at all.

From your encounters with the frog, the cow and the bunny,
You have learned that you are caring, smart and funny.
These things make you "You," not the spots on your back.
It doesn't matter how many you have or you lack."

Having no spots is just a part of being me.